CW01511967

In Pursuit of Pleasure

EPICURUS

In Pursuit of Pleasure

Translated by
Cyril Bailey

AIORA

Cyril Bailey (1871–1957) was an English classicist. He studied at Balliol College, Oxford, to where he returned as a fellow and tutor in 1902, and in 1933 was elected a fellow of the British Academy. His research focused on classical philosophers Lucretius and Epicurus.

Cover artwork: Panagiotis Stavropoulos
Ink on recycled paper produced by Kyra Stratoudaki.

EPICURUS: THE EXTANT REMAINS
Translated by Cyril Bailey (1926) pp.82-119.
By permission of Oxford University Press.

First edition May 2022

ISBN: 978-618-5369-57-6

AIORA PRESS
11 Mavromichali st.
Athens 10679 - Greece
tel: +30 210 3839000
www.aiorabooks.com

Contents

It is impossible to live a pleasant life
without living wisely and well and justly,
and it is impossible to live wisely
and well and justly
without living pleasantly.

E<small>PICURUS</small>

Preface

Epicurus was born in 341 BCE and was the son of Neocles, a schoolteacher, and Chaerestrate, both Athenians. He was brought up on Samos, his parents being among settlers sent there when Athens colonised the island. By Epicurus' own account he first came into contact with philosophy at the age of fourteen; it is said that he turned to philosophy in disgust at schoolmasters who could not explain the provenance of 'chaos' in Hesiod.[1]

Epicurus was exposed to the ideas of Plato and Democritus at an early age, under the teachers Pam-

---

[1] Hesiod's *Theogony* is Greece's first known creation story, according to which, at the beginning of all existence arose the formless void, Chaos.

philus of Samos, a Platonist, and Nausiphanes of Teos, a Democritean philosopher. In 323 BCE he came to Athens for the two-year military training required by the Athenian Constitution for all male Athenians at the age of eighteen before they could become citizens.[2] At that time Plato's Academy and Aristotle's Lyceum, both of which were then run by successors, were the two top schools of philosophy in Athens. Plato had died seven years before the birth of Epicurus and Xenocrates of Chalcedon was lecturing at the Academy. One account has Epicurus attending his lectures.[3] Theophrastus of Lesbos was teaching at the Lyceum, and Aristotle, the school's founder, had retired to Chalcis, where he died in 322 BCE.

The year Epicurus arrived in Athens, Alexander the Great died and shortly after Athens led a coali-

---

[2] It was in this service that Epicurus met and became friends with the poet Menander, who was born in the same year as himself.

[3] Demetrius the Magnesian, as cited in Diogenes Laertius, *Lives of Eminent Philosophers*, translated by R.D. Hicks, Cambridge MA: Harvard University Press, 1925. .

tion of cities in a revolt against Macedonian rule. In 322 BCE the coalition was defeated, and Athens was forced to surrender Samos. Athenian settlers were expelled and Epicurus' parents fled to Colophon on the coast of present-day Turkey. Epicurus joined them there, but for the next ten years little is known for certain about his life.

He began to teach when he was thirty-two, first in Mitylene on Lesbos and then in Lampsacus on the nearby mainland of present-day Turkey, where he gathered his first followers. In 306 BCE he moved to Athens with his loyal disciples, and bought a house with a garden where he established his school. The Garden, as the school came to be known, soon became popular among Athenian youth, alongside the Academy and the Lyceum. Notably, and in contrast to the other two schools, women and slaves were also admitted to the Garden.

Epicurus presented a complete philosophical system but was principally an ethical philosopher. He defined philosophy as 'a daily business of speech and thought to secure happiness', which he believed to be the goal of human life. He believed that happiness could be achieved through the pursuit of

pleasure. As proof he adduced the fact that 'living things, as soon as they are born, are well content with pleasure and are in enmity with pain, by the prompting of nature and apart from reason'. However, Epicurean philosophy was then and still is often misinterpreted as promoting hedonism. In fact, Epicurus considered pleasure to be connected to virtue rather than excess and sensual self-indulgence. According to Epicurus, virtue is the one thing without which pleasure cannot exist. In his famous *Letter to Menoeceus*, he affirms:

> When we say, then, that pleasure is the end and aim, we do not mean the pleasures of the prodigal or the pleasures of sensuality, as we are understood to do by some through ignorance, prejudice or willful misinterpretation. By pleasure we mean the absence of pain in the body and of trouble in the soul. It is not an unbroken succession of drinking-bouts and of revelry, not sexual love, not the enjoyment of the fish and other delicacies of a luxurious table, which produce a pleasant life; it is sober reasoning, searching out the grounds of every choice and avoidance, and banishing those

beliefs through which the greatest tumults take possession of the soul.

We are to choose virtues, he says, not for their own sake, but for the pleasure they give us, just as we take medicine for the sake of our health. The goal of a happy life, according to Epicurus, is attaining freedom from pain in the body (aponia) and from trouble in the mind (ataraxia), 'for it is to obtain this end that we always act, namely, to avoid pain and fear'. He holds mental pain to be worse than physical pain, as 'the flesh endures the storms of the present alone, while the mind those of the past and future as well as the present'. Consequently, he also holds mental pleasures to be greater than those of the body. He advocates for friendship, simple pleasures, contentment with one's lot and the renunciation of wealth and influence.

By the time of Epicurus' death in 270 BCE there were Epicurean schools in many cities of the Greek world. Hermarchus had studied under Epicurus and was the first to succeed him as head of the Garden, where the study of Epicurean philosophy continued uninterrupted until the fourth century

CE. In the second century BCE Epicureanism was brought to Rome, where it soon became popular, as shown by references to the philosophy in the work of Cicero and Seneca. Eventually, opposed both by Neoplatonists and the Fathers of the early Christian Church, it declined and had all but disappeared by the fifth century CE. Epicureanism remained in obscurity during the Middle Ages to be rediscovered during the Renaissance, when Italian humanist and Catholic priest Lorenzo Valla published a treatise on Epicurus entitled *De voluptate* [On pleasure].

Epicurus was a prolific author; he wrote approximately three hundred books or scrolls, but only a few fragments remain, as well as some letters. The main surviving source of information on him is *The Lives of Eminent Philosophers* written by third-century biographer Diogenes Laertius.[4] This work gives valuable details of Epicurus' life and insights

---

[4] *The Lives of Eminent Philosophers*, written in Greek and dated to the first half of the third century CE, is considered the most important surviving secondary source for the history of Greek philosophy. It contains invaluable information on nearly one hundred philosophers.

into his philosophy. It is also the only source for three complete letters of Epicurus, including the Letter to Menoeceus (Επιστολή προς Μενοικέα)[5], which provides a synopsis of Epicurean ethics, and the Principal Doctrines (Κύριαι δόξαι), a collection of aphorisms containing the essence of Epicurus' teachings, well known and highly respected in the antiquity as shown by the writings of Plutarch, Seneca and many others. Other sources of Epicurus' teachings include the Vatican Collection or Vatican Sayings, a collection of his quotations discovered in 1888 in a fourteenth-century manuscript in the Vatican Library; scrolls unearthed at the Villa of the Papyri at Herculaneum, in Campania, Italy; a number of third-century inscriptions on the walls

---

[5] The two other letters were written to Herodotus and Pythocles. The Letter to Herodotus is an obscure and complicated text setting out Epicurus' physical theory, while the Letter to Pythocles deals with astronomical phenomena and meteorology. In these three letters, according to Diogenes Laertius, Epicurus gave 'an epitome of his whole system'. More recent scholars, however, have questioned the authenticity of the Letter to Pythocles, which appears to be a compilation of different texts.

of the marketplace of Oenoanda, a provincial town in the heart of Asia Minor; and short passages from his works quoted by other authors.

This volume contains Cyril Bailey's masterly, classic translations of the most important surviving writing of Epicurus—the Letter to Menoeceus, the Principal Doctrines and the Vatican Collection—and offers the contemporary reader a comprehensive overview of Epicurean Ethics, his philosophy on what matters in life and how we should live.

Aris Laskaratos

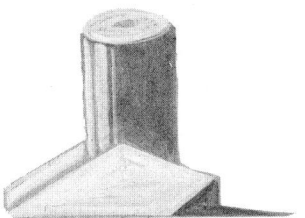

Ἐπιστολὴ πρὸς Μενοικέα

Letter to Menoeceus

Ἐπίκουρος Μενοικεῖ χαίρειν.

Μήτε νέος τις ὢν μελλέτω φιλοσοφεῖν, μήτε γέρων ὑπάρχων κοπιάτω φιλοσοφῶν. Οὔτε γὰρ ἄωρος οὐδείς ἐστιν οὔτε πάρωρος πρὸς τὸ κατὰ ψυχὴν ὑγιαῖνον. Ὁ δὲ λέγων ἢ μήπω τοῦ φιλοσοφεῖν ὑπάρχειν ἢ παρεληλυθέναι τὴν ὥραν, ὅμοιός ἐστιν τῷ λέγοντι πρὸς εὐ- δαιμονίαν ἢ μήπω παρεῖναι τὴν ὥραν ἢ μη- κέτ᾽ εἶναι. Ὥστε φιλοσοφητέον καὶ νέῳ καὶ γέροντι, τῷ μὲν ὅπως γηράσκων νεάζῃ τοῖς ἀγαθοῖς διὰ τὴν χάριν τῶν γεγονότων, τῷ δὲ ὅπως νέος ἅμα καὶ παλαιὸς ᾖ διὰ τὴν ἀφοβίαν

Epicurus to Menoeceus, greeting.

Let no one when young delay to study philosophy, nor when he is old grow weary of his study. For no one can come too early or too late to secure the health of his soul. And the man who says that the age for philosophy has either not yet come or has gone by is like the man who says that the age for happiness is not yet come to him, or has passed away. Wherefore both when young and old a man must study philosophy, that as he grows old he may be young in blessings through the grateful recollection of what has been, and that in youth he

τῶν μελλόντων· μελετᾶν οὖν χρὴ τὰ ποιοῦντα
τὴν εὐδαιμονίαν, εἴ περ παρούσης μὲν αὐτῆς
πάντα ἔχομεν, ἀπούσης δὲ πάντα πράττομεν
εἰς τὸ ταύτην ἔχειν.

Ἃ δέ σοι συνεχῶς παρήγγελλον, ταῦτα καὶ
πρᾶττε καὶ μελέτα, στοιχεῖα τοῦ καλῶς ζῆν
ταῦτ᾽ εἶναι διαλαμβάνων. Πρῶτον μὲν τὸν
θεὸν ζῷον ἄφθαρτον καὶ μακάριον νομίζων,
ὡς ἡ κοινὴ τοῦ θεοῦ νόησις ὑπεγράφη, μηθὲν μήτε τῆς ἀφθαρσίας ἀλλότριον μήτε τῆς
μακαριότητος ἀνοίκειον αὐτῷ πρόσαπτε· πᾶν
δὲ τὸ φυλάττειν αὐτοῦ δυνάμενον τὴν μετὰ
ἀφθαρσίας μακαριότητα περὶ αὐτὸν δόξα-
ζε. Θεοὶ μὲν γὰρ εἰσίν· ἐναργὴς γὰρ αὐτῶν
ἐστιν ἡ γνῶσις· οἵους δ᾽ αὐτοὺς <οἱ> πολλοὶ
νομίζουσιν, οὐκ εἰσίν· οὐ γὰρ φυλάττουσιν
αὐτοὺς οἵους νομίζουσιν. Ἀσεβὴς δὲ οὐχ ὁ
τοὺς τῶν πολλῶν θεοὺς ἀναιρῶν, ἀλλ᾽ ὁ τὰς
τῶν πολλῶν δόξας θεοῖς προσάπτων. Οὐ
γὰρ προλήψεις εἰσὶν ἀλλ᾽ ὑπολήψεις ψευδεῖς
αἱ τῶν πολλῶν ὑπὲρ θεῶν ἀποφάσεις, ἔνθεν
αἱ μέγισται βλάβαι ἐκ θεῶν ἐπάγονται καὶ

may be old as well, since he will know no fear of what is to come. We must then meditate on the things that make our happiness, seeing that when that is with us we have all, but when it is absent we do all to win it.

The things which I used unceasingly to commend to you, these do and practice, considering them to be the first principles of the good life. First of all believe that god is a being immortal and blessed, even as the common idea of a god is engraved on men's minds, and do not assign to him anything alien to his immortality or ill-suited to his blessedness: but believe about him everything that can uphold his blessedness and immortality. For gods there are, since the knowledge of them is by clear vision. But they are not such as the many believe them to be: for indeed they do not consistently represent them as they believe them to be. And the impious man is not he who denies the gods of the many, but he who attaches to the gods the beliefs of the many. For the statements of the many about the gods are not conceptions derived from

ὠφέλειαι <τοῖς ἀγαθοῖς>. Ταῖς γὰρ ἰδίαις οἰ-
κειούμενοι διὰ παντὸς ἀρεταῖς τοὺς ὁμοίους
ἀποδέχονται, πᾶν τὸ μὴ τοιοῦτον ὡς ἀλλότριον νομίζοντες.

Συνέθιζε δὲ ἐν τῷ νομίζειν μηδὲν πρὸς ἡμᾶς
εἶναι τὸν θάνατον· ἐπεὶ πᾶν ἀγαθὸν καὶ κακὸν
ἐν αἰσθήσει· στέρησις δέ ἐστιν αἰσθήσεως ὁ
θάνατος. Ὅθεν γνῶσις ὀρθὴ τοῦ μηθὲν εἶναι
πρὸς ἡμᾶς τὸν θάνατον ἀπολαυστὸν ποιεῖ τὸ
τῆς ζωῆς θνητόν, οὐκ ἄπειρον προστιθεῖσα
χρόνον, ἀλλὰ τὸν τῆς ἀθανασίας ἀφελομένη
πόθον. Οὐθὲν γάρ ἐστιν ἐν τῷ ζῆν δεινὸν τῷ
κατειληφότι γνησίως τὸ μηδὲν ὑπάρχειν ἐν τῷ
μὴ ζῆν δεινόν. Ὥστε μάταιος ὁ λέγων δεδιέ-
ναι τὸν θάνατον οὐχ ὅτι λυπήσει παρών, ἀλλ᾽
ὅτι λυπεῖ μέλλων. Ὁ γὰρ παρὸν οὐκ ἐνοχλεῖ,
προσδοκώμενον κενῶς λυπεῖ. Τὸ φρικωδέ-
στατον οὖν τῶν κακῶν ὁ θάνατος οὐθὲν πρὸς
ἡμᾶς, ἐπειδήπερ ὅταν μὲν ἡμεῖς ὦμεν, ὁ θάνατος οὐ πάρεστιν· ὅταν δ᾽ ὁ θάνατος παρῇ,
τόθ᾽ ἡμεῖς οὐκ ἐσμέν. Οὔτε οὖν πρὸς τοὺς ζῶ-
ντάς ἐστιν οὔτε πρὸς τοὺς τετελευτηκότας,

sensation, but false suppositions, according to which the greatest misfortunes befall the wicked and the greatest blessings (the good) by the gift of the gods. For men being accustomed always to their own virtues welcome those like themselves, but regard all that is not of their nature as alien.

Become accustomed to the belief that death is nothing to us. For all good and evil consists in sensation, but death is deprivation of sensation. And therefore a right understanding that death is nothing to us makes the mortality of life enjoyable, not because it adds to it an infinite span of time, but because it takes away the craving for immortality. For there is nothing terrible in life for the man who has truly comprehended that there is nothing terrible in not living. So that the man speaks but idly who says that he fears death not because it will be painful when it comes, but because it is painful in anticipation. For that which gives no trouble when it comes, is but an empty pain in anticipation. So death, the most terrifying of ills, is nothing to us, since so long as we exist, death is not with

ἐπειδήπερ περὶ οὓς μὲν οὐκ ἔστιν, οἳ δ᾽ οὐκέτι
εἰσίν.

Ἀλλ᾽ οἱ πολλοὶ τὸν θάνατον ὅτε μὲν ὡς μέγιστον τῶν κακῶν φεύγουσιν, ὅτε δὲ ὡς ἀνά-
παυσιν τῶν ἐν τῷ ζῆν <κακῶν ποθοῦσιν. Ὁ
δὲ σοφὸς οὔτε παραιτεῖται τὸ ζῆν> οὔτε φο-
βεῖται τὸ μὴ ζῆν· οὔτε γὰρ αὐτῷ προσίσταται
τὸ ζῆν οὔτε δοξάζεται κακὸν εἶναί τι τὸ μὴ ζῆν.
Ὥσπερ δὲ τὸ σιτίον οὐ τὸ πλεῖον πάντως ἀλλὰ
τὸ ἥδιστον αἱρεῖται, οὕτω καὶ χρόνον οὐ τὸν
μήκιστον ἀλλὰ τὸν ἥδιστον καρπίζεται.

Ὁ δὲ παραγγέλλων τὸν μὲν νέον καλῶς ζῆν,
τὸν δὲ γέροντα καλῶς καταστρέφειν εὐήθης
ἐστὶν οὐ μόνον διὰ τὸ τῆς ζωῆς ἀσπαστόν,
ἀλλὰ καὶ διὰ τὸ τὴν αὐτὴν εἶναι μελέτην τοῦ
καλῶς ζῆν καὶ τοῦ καλῶς ἀποθνήσκειν. Πολὺ
δὲ χείρων καὶ ὁ λέγων καλὸν μὲν μὴ φῦναι,
    φύντα δ᾽ ὅπως ὤκιστα πύλας Ἀίδαο περῆσαι.
Εἰ μὲν γὰρ πεποιθὼς τοῦτό φησι, πῶς οὐκ
ἀπέρχεται ἐκ τοῦ ζῆν; ἐν ἑτοίμῳ γὰρ αὐτῷ
τοῦτ᾽ ἐστίν, εἴ περ ἦν βεβουλευμένον αὐτῷ

us; but when death comes, then we do not exist. It does not then concern either the living or the dead, since for the former it is not, and the latter are no more.

But the many at one moment shun death as the greatest of evils, at another <yearn for it> as a respite from the <evils> in life. <But the wise man neither seeks to escape life> nor fears the cessation of life, for neither does life offend him nor does the absence of life seem to be any evil. And just as with food he does not seek simply the larger share and nothing else, but rather the most pleasant, so he seeks to enjoy not the longest period of time, but the most pleasant.

And he who counsels the young man to live well, but the old man to make a good end, is foolish, not merely because of the desirability of life, but also because it is the same training which teaches to live well and to die well. Yet much worse still is the man who says it is good not to be born, but 'once born make haste to pass the gates of Death'.

βεβαίως· εἰ δὲ μωκώμενος, μάταιος ἐν τοῖς οὐκ ἐπιδεχομένοις.

Μνημονευτέον δὲ ὡς τὸ μέλλον οὔτε ἡμέτερον οὔτε πάντως οὐχ ἡμέτερον, ἵνα μήτε πάντως προσμένωμεν ὡς ἐσόμενον μήτε ἀπελπίζωμεν ὡς πάντως οὐκ ἐσόμενον.

Ἀναλογιστέον δὲ ὡς τῶν ἐπιθυμιῶν αἱ μέν εἰσι φυσικαί, αἱ δὲ κεναί, καὶ τῶν φυσικῶν αἱ μὲν ἀναγκαῖαι, αἱ δὲ φυσικαὶ μόνον· τῶν δ' ἀναγκαίων αἱ μὲν πρὸς εὐδαιμονίαν εἰσὶν ἀναγκαῖαι, αἱ δὲ πρὸς τὴν τοῦ σώματος ἀοχλησίαν, αἱ δὲ πρὸς αὐτὸ τὸ ζῆν. Τούτων γὰρ ἀπλανὴς θεωρία πᾶσαν αἵρεσιν καὶ φυγὴν ἐπανάγειν οἶδεν ἐπὶ τὴν τοῦ σώματος ὑγίειαν καὶ τὴν <τῆς ψυχῆς> ἀταραξίαν, ἐπεὶ τοῦτο τοῦ μακαρίως ζῆν ἐστι τέλος. Τούτου γὰρ χάριν πάντα πράττομεν, ὅπως μήτε ἀλγῶμεν μήτε ταρβῶμεν. Ὅταν δὲ ἅπαξ τοῦτο περὶ ἡμᾶς γένηται, λύεται πᾶς ὁ τῆς ψυχῆς χειμών, οὐκ ἔχοντος τοῦ ζῴου βαδίζειν ὡς πρὸς ἐνδέον τι καὶ ζητεῖν ἕτερον ᾧ τὸ τῆς ψυχῆς

For if he says this from conviction why does he not pass away out of life? For it is open to him to do so, if he had firmly made up his mind to this. But if he speaks in jest, his words are idle among men who cannot receive them.

We must then bear in mind that the future is neither ours, nor yet wholly not ours, so that we may not altogether expect it as sure to come, nor abandon hope of it, as if it will certainly not come.

We must consider that of desires some are natural, others vain, and of the natural some are necessary and others merely natural; and of the necessary some are necessary for happiness, others for the repose of the body, and others for very life. The right understanding of these facts enables us to refer all choice and avoidance to the health of the body and <the soul's> freedom from disturbance, since this is the aim of the life of blessedness. For it is to obtain this end that we always act, namely, to avoid pain and fear. And when this is once secured for us, all the tempest of the soul is dispersed, since

καὶ τὸ τοῦ σώματος ἀγαθὸν συμπληρώσεται. Τότε γὰρ ἡδονῆς χρείαν ἔχομεν, ὅταν ἐκ τοῦ μὴ παρεῖναι τὴν ἡδονὴν ἀλγῶμεν· <ὅταν δὲ μὴ ἀλγῶμεν>, οὐκέτι τῆς ἡδονῆς δεόμεθα. Καὶ διὰ τοῦτο τὴν ἡδονὴν ἀρχὴν καὶ τέλος λέγομεν εἶναι τοῦ μακαρίως ζῆν· ταύτην γὰρ ἀγαθὸν πρῶτον καὶ συγγενικὸν ἔγνωμεν, καὶ ἀπὸ ταύτης καταρχόμεθα πάσης αἱρέσεως καὶ φυγῆς καὶ ἐπὶ ταύτην καταντῶμεν ὡς κανόνι τῷ πάθει πᾶν ἀγαθὸν κρίνοντες.

Καὶ ἐπεὶ πρῶτον ἀγαθὸν τοῦτο καὶ σύμφυτον, διὰ τοῦτο καὶ οὐ πᾶσαν ἡδονὴν αἱρούμεθα, ἀλλ᾽ ἔστιν ὅτε πολλὰς ἡδονὰς ὑπερβαίνομεν, ὅταν πλεῖον ἡμῖν τὸ δυσχερὲς ἐκ τούτων ἔπηται· καὶ πολλὰς ἀλγηδόνας ἡδονῶν κρείττους νομίζομεν, ἐπειδὰν μείζων ἡμῖν ἡδονὴ παρακολουθῇ πολὺν χρόνον ὑπομείνασι τὰς ἀλγηδόνας. Πᾶσα οὖν ἡδονὴ διὰ τὸ φύσιν ἔχειν οἰκείαν ἀγαθόν, οὐ πᾶσα μέντοι αἱρετή· καθάπερ καὶ ἀλγηδὼν πᾶσα κακόν, οὐ πᾶσα δὲ ἀεὶ φευκτὴ πεφυκυῖα. Τῇ μέντοι συμμετρήσει καὶ συμφερόντων καὶ ἀσυμφόρων βλέψει ταῦτα

the living creature has not to wander as though in search of something that is missing, and to look for some other thing by which he can fulfil the good of the soul and the good of the body. For it is then that we have need of pleasure, when we feel pain owing to the absence of pleasure; <but when we do not feel pain>, we no longer need pleasure. And for this cause we call pleasure the beginning and end of the blessed life. For we recognize pleasure as the first good innate in us, and from pleasure we begin every act of choice and avoidance, and to pleasure we return again, using the feeling as the standard by which we judge every good.

And since pleasure is the first good and natural to us, for this very reason we do not choose every pleasure, but sometimes we pass over many pleasures, when greater discomfort accrues to us as the result of them: and similarly we think many pains better than pleasures, since a greater pleasure comes to us when we have endured pains for a long time. Every pleasure then because of its natural kinship to us is good, yet not every pleasure is

πάντα κρίνειν καθήκει· χρώμεθα γὰρ τῷ μὲν ἀγαθῷ κατά τινας χρόνους ὡς κακῷ, τῷ δὲ κακῷ τοὔμπαλιν ὡς ἀγαθῷ.

Καὶ τὴν αὐτάρκειαν δὲ ἀγαθὸν μέγα νομίζομεν, οὐχ ἵνα πάντως τοῖς ὀλίγοις χρώμεθα, ἀλλ᾽ ὅπως ἐὰν μὴ ἔχωμεν τὰ πολλά, τοῖς ὀλίγοις χρώμεθα, πεπεισμένοι γνησίως ὅτι ἥδιστα πολυτελείας ἀπολαύουσιν οἱ ἥκιστα ταύτης δεόμενοι, καὶ ὅτι τὸ μὲν φυσικὸν πᾶν εὐπόριστόν ἐστι, τὸ δὲ κενὸν δυσπόριστον. Οἵ τε λιτοὶ χυλοὶ ἴσην πολυτελεῖ διαίτῃ τὴν ἡδονὴν ἐπιφέρουσιν, ὅταν ἅπαν τὸ ἀλγοῦν κατ᾽ ἔνδειαν ἐξαιρεθῇ· καὶ μᾶζα καὶ ὕδωρ τὴν ἀκροτάτην ἀποδίδωσιν ἡδονήν, ἐπειδὰν ἐνδέων τις αὐτὰ προσενέγκηται. Τὸ συνεθίζειν οὖν ἐν ταῖς ἁπλαῖς καὶ οὐ πολυτελέσι διαίταις καὶ ὑγιείας ἐστὶ συμπληρωτικὸν καὶ πρὸς τὰς ἀναγκαίας τοῦ βίου χρήσεις ἄοκνον ποιεῖ τὸν ἄνθρωπον καὶ τοῖς πολυτελέσιν ἐκ διαλειμμάτων προσερχομένους κρεῖττον ἡμᾶς διατίθησι καὶ πρὸς τὴν τύχην ἀφόβους παρασκευάζει.

to be chosen: even as every pain also is an evil, yet not all are always of a nature to be avoided. Yet by a scale of comparison and by the consideration of advantages and disadvantages we must form our judgement on all these matters. For the good on certain occasions we treat as bad, and conversely the bad as good.

And again independence of desire we think a great good—not that we may at all times enjoy but a few things, but that, if we do not possess many, we may enjoy the few in the genuine persuasion that those have the sweetest pleasure in luxury who least need it, and that all that is natural is easy to be obtained, but that which is superfluous is hard. And so plain savours bring us a pleasure equal to a luxurious diet, when all the pain due to want is removed; and bread and water produce the highest pleasure, when one who needs them puts them to his lips. To grow accustomed therefore to simple and not luxurious diet gives us health to the full, and makes a man alert for the needful employments of life, and when after long intervals we

Ὅταν οὖν λέγωμεν ἡδονὴν τέλος ὑπάρχειν, οὐ τὰς τῶν ἀσώτων ἡδονὰς καὶ τὰς ἐν ἀπολαύσει κειμένας λέγομεν, ὥς τινες ἀγνοοῦντες καὶ οὐχ ὁμολογοῦντες ἢ κακῶς ἐκδεχόμενοι νομίζουσιν, ἀλλὰ τὸ μήτε ἀλγεῖν κατὰ σῶμα μήτε ταράττεσθαι κατὰ ψυχήν. Οὐ γὰρ πότοι καὶ κῶμοι συνείροντες οὐδ᾽ ἀπολαύσεις παίδων καὶ γυναικῶν οὐδ᾽ ἰχθύων καὶ τῶν ἄλλων, ὅσα φέρει πολυτελὴς τράπεζα, τὸν ἡδὺν γεννᾷ βίον, ἀλλὰ νήφων λογισμὸς καὶ τὰς αἰτίας ἐξερευνῶν πάσης αἱρέσεως καὶ φυγῆς καὶ τὰς δόξας ἐξελαύνων, ἐξ ὧν πλεῖστος τὰς ψυχὰς καταλαμβάνει θόρυβος.

Τούτων δὲ πάντων ἀρχὴ καὶ τὸ μέγιστον ἀγαθὸν φρόνησις· διὸ καὶ φιλοσοφίας τιμιώτερον ὑπάρχει φρόνησις, ἐξ ἧς αἱ λοιπαὶ πᾶσαι πεφύκασιν ἀρεταί, διδάσκουσα ὡς οὐκ ἔστιν ἡδέως ζῆν ἄνευ τοῦ φρονίμως καὶ καλῶς καὶ δικαίως <οὐδὲ φρονίμως καὶ καλῶς καὶ δικαίως> ἄνευ τοῦ ἡδέως· συμπεφύκασι γὰρ αἱ ἀρεταὶ τῷ ζῆν ἡδέως, καὶ τὸ ζῆν ἡδέως τούτων ἐστὶν ἀχώριστον. Ἐπεὶ τίνα νομίζεις

approach luxuries disposes us better towards them, and fits us to be fearless of fortune.

When, therefore, we maintain that pleasure is the end, we do not mean the pleasures of profligates and those that consist in sensuality, as is supposed by some who are either ignorant or disagree with us or do not understand, but freedom from pain in the body and from trouble in the mind. For it is not continuous drinkings and revellings, nor the satisfaction of lusts, nor the enjoyment of fish and other luxuries of the wealthy table, which produce a pleasant life, but sober reasoning, searching out the motives for all choice and avoidance, and banishing mere opinions, to which are due the greatest disturbance of the spirit.

Of all this the beginning and the greatest good is prudence. Wherefore prudence is a more precious thing even than philosophy: for from prudence are sprung all the other virtues, and it teaches us that it is not possible to live pleasantly without living prudently and honourably and justly, <nor, again,

εἶναι κρείττονα τοῦ καὶ περὶ θεῶν ὅσια δοξά-
ζοντος καὶ περὶ θανάτου διὰ παντὸς ἀφόβως
ἔχοντος καὶ τὸ τῆς φύσεως ἐπιλελογισμένου
τέλος, καὶ τὸ μὲν τῶν ἀγαθῶν πέρας ὡς ἔστιν
εὐσυμπλήρωτόν τε καὶ εὐπόριστον διαλαμ-
βάνοντος, τὸ δὲ τῶν κακῶν ὡς ἢ χρόνους ἢ
πόνους ἔχει βραχεῖς, τὴν δὲ ὑπό τινων δεσπό-
τιν εἰσαγομένην πάντων ἐγγελῶντος <εἱμαρ-
μένην; ὧν ἃ μὲν κατ' ἀνάγκην γίνεται>, ἃ δὲ
ἀπὸ τύχης, ἃ δὲ παρ' ἡμᾶς διὰ τὸ τὴν μὲν
ἀνάγκην ἀνυπεύθυνον εἶναι, τὴν δὲ τύχην
ἄστατον ὁρᾶν, τὸ δὲ παρ' ἡμᾶς ἀδέσποτον,
ᾧ καὶ τὸ μεμπτὸν καὶ τὸ ἐναντίον παρακο-
λουθεῖν πέφυκεν <ἐπεὶ κρεῖττον ἦν τῷ περὶ
θεῶν μύθῳ κατακολουθεῖν ἢ τῇ τῶν φυσικῶν
εἱμαρμένῃ δουλεύειν· ὁ μὲν γὰρ ἐλπίδα πα-
ραιτήσεως ὑπογράφει θεῶν διὰ τιμῆς, ἡ δὲ
ἀπαραίτητον ἔχει τὴν ἀνάγκην>, τὴν δὲ τύχην οὔτε θεὸν, ὡς οἱ πολλοὶ νομίζουσιν, ὑπο-
λαμβάνων (οὐθὲν γὰρ ἀτάκτως θεῷ πράττε-
ται) οὔτε <πάντων> ἀβέβαιον αἰτίαν (<οὐκ>
οἴεται μὲν γὰρ ἀγαθὸν ἢ κακὸν ἐκ ταύτης
πρὸς τὸ μακαρίως ζῆν ἀνθρώποις δίδοσθαι,

to live a life of prudence, honour, and justice> without living pleasantly. For the virtues are by nature bound up with the pleasant life, and the pleasant life is inseparable from them. For indeed who, think you, is a better man than he who holds reverent opinions concerning the gods, and is at all times free from fear of death, and has reasoned out the end ordained by nature? He understands that the limit of good things is easy to fulfil and easy to attain, whereas the course of ills is either short in time or slight in pain: he laughs at <destiny>, whom some have introduced as the mistress of all things. <He thinks that with us lies the chief power in determining events, some of which happen by necessity> and some by chance, and some are within our control; for while necessity cannot be called to account, he sees that chance is inconstant, but that which is in our control is subject to no master, and to it are naturally attached praise and blame. For, indeed, it were better to follow the myths about the gods than to become a slave to the destiny of the natural philosophers: for the former suggests a hope of placating the gods by worship,

ἀρχὰς μέντοι μεγάλων ἀγαθῶν ἢ κακῶν ὑπὸ
ταύτης χορηγεῖσθαι), κρεῖττον εἶναι νομίζει
εὐλογίστως ἀτυχεῖν ἢ ἀλογίστως εὐτυχεῖν·
(βέλτιον γὰρ ἐν ταῖς πράξεσι τὸ καλῶς κριθὲν
<σφαλῆναι μᾶλλον ἢ το κακῶς κριθὲν> ὀρ-
θωθῆναι διὰ ταύτην).

Ταῦτα οὖν καὶ τὰ τούτοις συγγενῆ μελέτα
πρὸς σεαυτὸν ἡμέρας καὶ νυκτὸς πρός <τε>
τὸν ὅμοιον σεαυτῷ, καὶ οὐδέποτε οὔθ' ὕπαρ
οὔτ' ὄναρ διαταραχθήσῃ, ζήσεις δὲ ὡς θεὸς
ἐν ἀνθρώποις. Οὐθὲν γὰρ ἔοικε θνητῷ ζώῳ
ζῶν ἄνθρωπος ἐν ἀθανάτοις ἀγαθοῖς.

whereas the latter involves a necessity which knows no placation As to chance, he does not regard it as a god as most men do (for in a god's acts there is no disorder), nor as an uncertain cause <of all things>; for he does not believe that good and evil are given by chance to man for the framing of a blessed life, but that opportunities for great good and great evil are afforded by it. He therefore thinks it better to be unfortunate in reasonable action than to prosper in unreason. For it is better in a man's actions that what is well chosen <should fail, rather than that what is ill chosen> should be successful owing to chance.

Meditate therefore on these things and things akin to them night and day by yourself; and with a companion like to yourself, and never shall you be disturbed waking or asleep, but you shall live like a god among men. For a man who lives among immortal blessings is not like to a mortal being.

Κύριαι δόξαι

Principal Doctrines

I. Τὸ μακάριον καὶ ἄφθαρτον οὔτε αὐτὸ πράγματα ἔχει οὔτε ἄλλῳ παρέχει, ὥστε οὔτε ὀργαῖς οὔτε χάρισι συνέχεται· ἐν ἀσθενεῖ γὰρ πᾶν τὸ τοιοῦτον.

II. Ὁ θάνατος οὐδὲν πρὸς ἡμᾶς· τὸ γὰρ διαλυθὲν ἀναισθητεῖ· τὸ δ' ἀναισθητοῦν οὐδὲν πρὸς ἡμᾶς.

III. Ὅρος τοῦ μεγέθους τῶν ἡδονῶν ἡ παντὸς τοῦ ἀλγοῦντος ὑπεξαίρεσις. Ὅπου δ' ἂν τὸ ἡδόμενον ἐνῇ, καθ' ὃν ἂν χρόνον ᾖ, οὐκ ἔστι τὸ ἀλγοῦν ἢ τὸ λυπούμενον ἢ τὸ συναμφότερον.

I. The blessed and immortal nature knows no trouble itself nor causes trouble to any other, so that it is never constrained by anger or favour. For all such things exist only in the weak.

II. Death is nothing to us; for that which is dissolved is without sensation; and that which lacks sensation is nothing to us.

III. The limit of quantity in pleasures is the removal of all that is painful. Wherever pleasure is present, as long as it is there, there is neither pain of body nor of mind, nor of both at once.

IV. Οὐ χρονίζει τὸ ἀλγοῦν συνεχῶς ἐν τῇ σαρ-
κί, ἀλλὰ τὸ μὲν ἄκρον τὸν ἐλάχιστον χρόνον πάρεστι, τὸ δὲ μόνον ὑπερτεῖνον τὸ
ἡδόμενον κατὰ σάρκα οὐ πολλὰς ἡμέρας
συμβαίνει· αἱ δὲ πολυχρόνιοι τῶν ἀρρω-
στιῶν πλεονάζον ἔχουσι τὸ ἡδόμενον ἐν τῇ
σαρκὶ ἤ περ τὸ ἀλγοῦν.

V. Οὐκ ἔστιν ἡδέως ζῆν ἄνευ τοῦ φρονίμως
καὶ καλῶς καὶ δικαίως <οὐδὲ φρονίμως καὶ
καλῶς καὶ δικαίως> ἄνευ τοῦ ἡδέως· ὅτῳ
δὲ τοῦτο μὴ ὑπάρχει, οὐ ζῇ φρονίμως καὶ
καλῶς καὶ δικαίως, <καὶ ὅτῳ ἐκεῖνο μὴ>
ὑπάρχει, οὐκ ἔστι τοῦτον ἡδέως ζῆν.

VI. Ἕνεκα τοῦ θαρρεῖν ἐξ ἀνθρώπων ἦν κατὰ
φύσιν ἀγαθόν, ἐξ ὧν ἄν ποτε τοῦτο οἷός τ' ἦ
παρασκευάζεσθαι.

VII. Ἔνδοξοι καὶ περίβλεπτοί τινες ἐβουλήθη-
σαν γενέσθαι, τὴν ἐξ ἀνθρώπων ἀσφάλειαν
οὕτω νομίζοντες περιποιήσεσθαι. Ὥστε εἰ
μὲν ἀσφαλὴς ὁ τῶν τοιούτων βίος, ἀπέλα-

IV. Pain does not last continuously in the flesh, but the acutest pain is there for a very short time, and even that which just exceeds the pleasure in the flesh does not continue for many days at once. But chronic illnesses permit a predominance of pleasure over pain in the flesh.

V. It is not possible to live pleasantly without living prudently and honourably and justly, [nor again to live a life of prudence, honour, and Justice] without living pleasantly. And the man who does not possess the pleasant life, is not living prudently and honourably and justly, [and the man who does not possess the virtuous life], cannot possibly live pleasantly.

VI. To secure protection from men anything is a natural good, by which you may be able to attain this end.

VII. Some men wished to become famous and conspicuous, thinking that they would thus win for themselves safety from other men. Wherefore if

βον τὸ τῆς φύσεως ἀγαθόν· εἰ δὲ μὴ ἀσφα-
λής, οὐκ ἔχουσιν οὗ ἕνεκα ἐξ ἀρχῆς κατὰ τὸ
τῆς φύσεως οἰκεῖον ὠρέχθησαν.

VIII. Οὐδεμία ἡδονὴ καθ᾽ ἑαυτὸ κακόν· ἀλλὰ τὰ
τινῶν ἡδονῶν ποιητικὰ πολλαπλασίους ἐπι-
φέρει τὰς ὀχλήσεις τῶν ἡδονῶν.

IX. Εἰ κατεπυκνοῦτο πᾶσα ἡδονή, καὶ χρόνῳ
καὶ περὶ ὅλον τὸ ἄθροισμα ὑπῆρχεν ἢ τὰ κυριώτατα μέρη τῆς φύσεως, οὐκ ἄν ποτε διέ-
φερον ἀλλήλων αἱ ἡδοναί.

X. Εἰ τὰ ποιητικὰ τῶν περὶ τοὺς ἀσώτους ἡδονῶν ἔλυε τοὺς φόβους τῆς διανοίας τούς τε
περὶ μετεώρων καὶ θανάτου καὶ ἀλγηδόνων,
ἔτι τε τὸ πέρας τῶν ἐπιθυμιῶν <καὶ τῶν ἀλ-
γηδόνων> ἐδίδασκεν, οὐκ ἄν ποτε εἴχομεν ὅ
τι μεμψαίμεθα αὐτοῖς, πανταχόθεν ἐκπλη-
ρουμένοις τῶν ἡδονῶν καὶ οὐδαμόθεν οὔτε
τὸ ἀλγοῦν οὔτε τὸ λυπούμενον ἔχουσιν, ὅ-
περ ἐστὶ τὸ κακόν.

the life of such men is safe, they have obtained the good which nature craves; but if it is not safe, they do not possess that for which they strove at first by the instinct of nature.

VIII. No pleasure is a bad thing in itself: but the means which produce some pleasures bring with them disturbances many times greater than the pleasures.

IX. If every pleasure could be intensified so that it lasted and influenced the whole organism or the most essential parts of our nature, pleasures would never differ from one another.

X. If the things that produce the pleasures of profligates could dispel the fears of the mind about the phenomena of the sky and death and its pains, and also teach the limits of desires <and of pains>, we should never have cause to blame them: for they would be filling themselves full with pleasures from every source and never have pain of body or mind, which is the evil of life.

XI. Εἰ μηθὲν ἡμᾶς αἱ τῶν μετεώρων ὑποψίαι ἠνώχλουν καὶ αἱ περὶ θανάτου, μή ποτε πρὸς ἡμᾶς ᾖ τι, ἔτι τε τὸ μὴ κατανοεῖν τοὺς ὅρους τῶν ἀλγηδόνων καὶ τῶν ἐπιθυμιῶν, οὐκ ἂν προσεδεόμεθα φυσιολογίας.

XII. Οὐκ ἦν τὸ φοβούμενον λύειν ὑπὲρ τῶν κυριωτάτων μὴ κατειδότα τίς ἡ τοῦ σύμπαντος φύσις, ἀλλ᾽ ὑποπτευόμενόν τι τῶν κατὰ τοὺς μύθους. Ὥστε οὐκ ἦν ἄνευ φυσιολογίας ἀκεραίους τὰς ἡδονὰς ἀπολαμβάνειν.

XIII. Οὐθὲν ὄφελος ἦν τὴν κατ᾽ ἀνθρώπους ἀσφάλειαν κατασκευάζεσθαι τῶν ἄνωθεν ὑπόπτων καθεστώτων καὶ τῶν ὑπὸ γῆς καὶ ἁπλῶς τῶν ἐν τῷ ἀπείρῳ.

XIV. Τῆς ἀσφαλείας τῆς ἐξ ἀνθρώπων γενομένης μέχρι τινὸς δυνάμει τινὶ ἐξοριστικῇ καὶ εὐπορίᾳ εἰλικρινεστάτη γίνεται ἡ ἐκ τῆς ἡσυχίας καὶ ἐκχωρήσεως τῶν πολλῶν ἀσφάλεια.

XI. If we were not troubled by our suspicions of the phenomena of the sky and about death, fearing that it concerns us, and also by our failure to grasp the limits of pains and desires, we should have no need of natural science.

XII. A man cannot dispel his fear about the most important matters if he does not know what is the nature of the universe but suspects the truth of some mythical story. So that without natural science it is not possible to attain our pleasures unalloyed.

XIII. There is no profit in securing protection in relation to men, if things above and things beneath the earth and indeed all in the boundless universe remain matters of suspicion.

XIV. The most unalloyed source of protection from men, which is secured to some extent by a certain force of expulsion, is in fact the immunity which results from a quiet life and the retirement from the world.

XV. Ὁ τῆς φύσεως πλοῦτος καὶ ὥρισται καὶ εὐπόριστός ἐστιν· ὁ δὲ τῶν κενῶν δοξῶν εἰς ἄπειρον ἐκπίπτει.

XVI. Βραχέα σοφῷ τύχη παρεμπίπτει, τὰ δὲ μέγιστα καὶ κυριώτατα ὁ λογισμὸς διῴκησε καὶ κατὰ τὸν συνεχῆ χρόνον τοῦ βίου διοικεῖ καὶ διοικήσει.

XVII. Ὁ δίκαιος ἀταρακτότατος, ὁ δ᾽ ἄδικος πλείστης ταραχῆς γέμων.

XVIII. Οὐκ ἐπαύξεται ἐν τῇ σαρκὶ ἡ ἡδονή, ἐπειδὰν ἅπαξ τὸ κατ᾽ ἔνδειαν ἀλγοῦν ἐξαιρεθῇ, ἀλλὰ μόνον ποικίλλεται· τῆς δὲ διανοίας τὸ πέρας τὸ κατὰ τὴν ἡδονὴν ἀπεγέννησεν ἥ τε τούτων αὐτῶν ἐκλόγισις καὶ τῶν ὁμογενῶν τούτοις, ὅσα τοὺς μεγίστους φόβους παρεσκεύαζε τῇ διανοίᾳ.

XIX. Ὁ ἄπειρος χρόνος ἴσην ἔχει τὴν ἡδονὴν καὶ ὁ πεπερασμένος, ἐάν τις αὐτῆς τὰ πέρατα καταμετρήσῃ τῷ λογισμῷ.

XV. The wealth demanded by nature is both limited and easily procured; that demanded by idle imaginings stretches on to infinity.

XVI. In but few things chance hinders a wise man, but the greatest and most important matters reason has ordained and throughout the whole period of life does and will ordain.

XVII. The just man is most free from trouble, the unjust most full of trouble.

XVIII. The pleasure in the flesh is not increased, when once the pain due to want is removed, but is only varied: and the limit as regards pleasure in the mind is begotten by the reasoned understanding of these very pleasures and of the emotions akin to them, which used to cause the greatest fear to the mind.

XIX. Infinite time contains no greater pleasure than limited time, if one measures by reason the limits of pleasure.

XX. Ἡ μὲν σὰρξ ἀπέλαβε τὰ πέρατα τῆς ἡδονῆς ἄπειρα, καὶ ἄπειρος αὐτὴν χρόνος παρεσκεύασεν. Ἡ δὲ διάνοια τοῦ τῆς σαρκὸς
τέλους καὶ πέρατος λαβοῦσα τὸν ἐπιλογι-
σμὸν, καὶ τοὺς ὑπὲρ τοῦ αἰῶνος φόβους
ἐκλύσασα τὸν παντελῆ βίον παρεσκεύασεν,
καὶ οὐθὲν ἔτι τοῦ ἀπείρου χρόνου προσεδε-
ήθημεν· ἀλλ᾽ οὔτε ἔφυγε τὴν ἡδονὴν οὔθ᾽
ἡνίκα τὴν ἐξαγωγὴν ἐκ τοῦ ζῆν τὰ πράγματα παρεσκεύαζεν, ὡς ἐλλείπουσά τι τοῦ
ἀρίστου βίου κατέστρεφεν.

XXI. Ὁ τὰ πέρατα τοῦ βίου κατειδὼς οἶδεν ὡς
εὐπόριστόν ἐστι τὸ <τὸ> ἀλγοῦν κατ᾽ ἔνδειαν ἐξαιροῦν καὶ τὸ τὸν ὅλον βίον παντελῆ καθιστάν· ὥστε οὐδὲν προσδεῖται πραγμάτων ἀγῶνας κεκτημένων.

XXII. Τὸ ὑφεστηκὸς δεῖ τέλος ἐπιλογίζεσθαι
καὶ πᾶσαν τὴν ἐνάργειαν, ἐφ᾽ ἣν τὰ δοξαζό-
μενα ἀνάγομεν· εἰ δὲ μὴ, πάντα ἀκρισίας καὶ
ταραχῆς ἔσται μεστά.

XX. The flesh perceives the limits of pleasure as unlimited and unlimited time is required to supply it. But the mind, having attained a reasoned understanding of the ultimate good of the flesh and its limits and having dissipated the fears concerning the time to come, supplies us with the complete life, and we have no further need of infinite time: but neither does the mind shun pleasure, nor, when circumstances begin to bring about the departure from life, does it approach its end as though it fell short in any way of the best life.

XXI. He who has learned the limits of life knows that that which removes the pain due to want and makes the whole of life complete is easy to obtain; so that there is no need of actions which involve competition.

XXII. We must consider both the real purpose and all the evidence of direct perception, to which we always refer the conclusions of opinion; otherwise, all will be full of doubt and confusion.

XXIII. Εἰ μάχῃ πάσαις ταῖς αἰσθήσεσιν, οὐχ ἕ-
ξεις οὐδ' ἃς ἂν φῇς αὐτῶν διεψεῦσθαι πρὸς
τί ποιούμενος τὴν ἀναγωγὴν κρίνῃς.

XXIV. Εἰ τιν' ἐκβαλεῖς ἁπλῶς αἴσθησιν καὶ μὴ
διαιρήσεις τὸ δοξαζόμενον κατὰ τὸ προσμένον καὶ τὸ παρὸν ἤδη κατὰ τὴν αἴσθησιν καὶ τὰ πάθη καὶ πᾶσαν φανταστικὴν
ἐπιβολὴν τῆς διανοίας, συνταράξεις καὶ τὰς
λοιπὰς αἰσθήσεις τῇ ματαίῳ δόξῃ, ὥστε τὸ
κριτήριον ἅπαν ἐκβαλεῖς. Εἰ δὲ βεβαιώσεις
καὶ τὸ προσμένον ἅπαν ἐν ταῖς δοξαστικαῖς
ἐννοίαις καὶ τὸ μὴ τὴν ἐπιμαρτύρησιν, οὐκ
ἐκλείψεις τὸ διεψευσμένον, ὡς τετηρηκὼς
ἔσει πᾶσαν ἀμφισβήτησιν καὶ πᾶσαν κρίσιν
τοῦ ὀρθῶς ἢ μὴ ὀρθῶς.

XXV. Εἰ μὴ παρὰ πάντα καιρὸν ἐπανοίσεις
ἕκαστον τῶν πραττομένων ἐπὶ τὸ τέλος
τῆς φύσεως, ἀλλὰ προκαταστρέψεις εἴτε
φυγὴν εἴτε δίωξιν ποιούμενος εἰς ἄλλό τι,
οὐκ ἔσονταί σοι τοῖς λόγοις αἱ πράξεις ἀκό-
λουθοι.

XXIII. If you fight against all sensations, you will have no standard by which to judge even those of them which you say are false.

XXIV. If you reject any single sensation and fail to distinguish between the conclusion of opinion as to the appearance awaiting confirmation and that which is actually given by the sensation or feeling, or each intuitive apprehension of the mind, you will confound all other sensations as well with the same groundless opinion, so that you will reject every standard of judgement. And if among the mental images created by your opinion you affirm both that which awaits confirmation and that which does not, you will not escape error, since you will have preserved the whole cause of doubt in every judgement between what is right and what is wrong.

XXV. If on each occasion Instead of referring your actions to the end of nature, you turn to some other nearer standard when you are making a

XXVI. Τῶν ἐπιθυμιῶν ὅσαι μὴ ἐπ᾽ ἀλγοῦν ἐπανάγουσιν, ἐὰν μὴ συμπληρωθῶσιν, οὐκ εἰσὶν ἀναγκαῖαι ἀλλ᾽ εὐδιάχυτον τὴν ὄρεξιν ἔχουσιν, ὅταν δυσπορίστων <ἦ> ἢ βλάβης ἀπεργαστικαὶ δόξωσιν εἶναι.

XXVII. Ὧν ἡ σοφία παρασκευάζεται εἰς τὴν τοῦ ὅλου βίου μακαριότητα, πολὺ μέγιστόν ἐστιν ἡ τῆς φιλίας κτῆσις.

XXVIII. Ἡ αὐτὴ γνώμη θαρρεῖν τε ἐποίησεν ὑπὲρ τοῦ μηθὲν αἰώνιον εἶναι δεινὸν μηδὲ πολυχρόνιον, καὶ τὴν ἐν αὐτοῖς τοῖς ὡρισμένοις ἀσφάλειαν φιλίας μάλιστα κατεῖδε συντελουμένην.

XXIX. Τῶν ἐπιθυμιῶν αἱ μέν εἰσι φυσικαὶ καὶ <ἀναγκαῖαι· αἱ δὲ φυσικαὶ μὲν> οὐκ ἀναγκαῖαι <δὲ>· αἱ δὲ οὔτε φυσικαὶ οὔτε ἀναγκαῖαι ἀλλὰ παρὰ κενὴν δόξαν γινόμεναι.

choice or an avoidance, your actions will not be consistent with your principles.

XXVI. Of desires, all that do not lead to a sense of pain, if they are not satisfied, are not necessary, but involve a craving which is easily dispelled, when the object is hard to procure or they seem likely to produce harm.

XXVII. Of all the things which wisdom acquires to produce the blessedness of the complete life, far the greatest is the possession of friendship.

XXVIII. The same conviction which has given us confidence that there is nothing terrible that lasts for ever or even for long, has also seen the protection of friendship most fully completed in the limited evils of this life.

XXIX. Among desires some are natural <and necessary, some natural> but not necessary, and others neither natural nor necessary, but due to idle imagination.

XXX. Ἐν αἷς τῶν φυσικῶν ἐπιθυμιῶν, μὴ ἐπ᾽ ἀλγοῦν δὲ ἐπαναγουσῶν, ἐὰν μὴ συντελεσθῶσιν, ὑπάρχει ἡ σπουδὴ σύντονος, παρὰ κενὴν δόξαν αὗται γίνονται, καὶ οὐ παρὰ τὴν ἑαυτῶν φύσιν οὐ διαχέονται ἀλλὰ παρὰ τὴν τοῦ ἀνθρώπου κενοδοξίαν.

XXXI. Τὸ τῆς φύσεως δίκαιον ἐστὶ σύμβολον τοῦ συμφέροντος εἰς τὸ μὴ βλάπτειν ἀλλήλους μηδὲ βλάπτεσθαι.

XXXII. Ὅσα τῶν ζῴων μὴ ἐδύνατο συνθήκας ποιεῖσθαι τὰς ὑπὲρ τοῦ μὴ βλάπτειν ἄλληλα μηδὲ βλάπτεσθαι, πρὸς ταῦτα οὐθὲν ἦν δίκαιον οὐδὲ ἄδικον· ὡσαύτως δὲ καὶ τῶν ἐθνῶν ὅσα μὴ ἐδύνατο ἢ μὴ ἐβούλετο τὰς συνθήκας ποιεῖσθαι τὰς ὑπὲρ τοῦ μὴ βλάπτειν μηδὲ βλάπτεσθαι.

XXX. Wherever in the case of desires which are physical, but do not lead to a sense of pain, if they are not fulfilled, the effort is intense, such pleasures are due to idle imagination, and it is not owing to their own nature that they fail to be dispelled, but owing to the empty imaginings of the man.

XXXI. The justice which arises from nature is a pledge of mutual advantage to restrain men from harming one another and save them from being harmed.

XXXII. For all living things which have not been able to make compacts not to harm one another or be harmed, nothing ever is either just or unjust; and likewise too for all tribes of men which have been unable or unwilling to make compacts not to harm or be harmed.

XXXIII. Οὐκ ἦν τι καθ᾽ ἑαυτὸ δικαιοσύνη, ἀλλ᾽ ἐν ταῖς μετ᾽ ἀλλήλων συστροφαῖς καθ᾽ ὁπηλίκους δή ποτε ἀεὶ τόπους συνθήκη τις ὑπὲρ τοῦ μὴ βλάπτειν ἢ βλάπτεσθαι.

XXXIV. Ἡ ἀδικία οὐ καθ᾽ ἑαυτὴν κακόν, ἀλλ᾽ ἐν τῷ κατὰ τὴν ὑποψίαν φόβῳ, εἰ μὴ λήσει τοὺς ὑπὲρ τῶν τοιούτων ἐφεστηκότας κολαστάς.

XXXV. Οὐκ ἔστι τὸν λάθρα τι ποιοῦντα ὧν συνέθεντο πρὸς ἀλλήλους εἰς τὸ μὴ βλάπτειν μηδὲ βλάπτεσθαι, πιστεύειν ὅτι λήσει, κἂν μυριάκις ἐπὶ τοῦ παρόντος λανθάνῃ. Μέχρι γὰρ καταστροφῆς ἄδηλον εἰ καὶ λήσει.

XXXVI. Κατὰ μὲν <τὸ> κοινὸν πᾶσι τὸ δίκαιον τὸ αὐτό, συμφέρον γάρ τι ἦν ἐν τῇ πρὸς ἀλλήλους κοινωνίᾳ· κατὰ δὲ τὸ ἴδιον χώρας καὶ ὅσων δή ποτε αἰτίων οὐ πᾶσι συνέπεται τὸ αὐτὸ δίκαιον εἶναι.

XXXIII. Justice never is anything in itself, but in the dealings of men with one another in any place whatever and at any time it is a kind of compact not to harm or be harmed.

XXXIV. Injustice is not an evil in itself, but only in consequence of the fear which attaches to the apprehension of being unable to escape those appointed to punish such actions.

XXXV. It is not possible for one who acts in secret contravention of the terms of the compact not to harm or be harmed, to be confident that he will escape detection, even if at present he escapes a thousand times. For up to the time of death it cannot be certain that he will indeed escape.

XXXVI. In its general aspect justice is the same for all, for it is a kind of mutual advantage in the dealings of men with one another: but with reference to the individual peculiarities of a country or any other circumstances the same thing does not turn out to be just for all.

XXXVII. Τὸ μὲν ἐπιμαρτυρούμενον ὅτι συμφέρει ἐν ταῖς χρείαις τῆς πρὸς ἀλλήλους κοινωνίας τῶν νομισθέντων εἶναι δικαίων, ἔχει τὸν τοῦ δικαίου ἐνέχυρον, ἐάν τε τὸ αὐτὸ πᾶσι γένηται, ἐάν τε μὴ τὸ αὐτό. Ἐὰν δὲ νόμον θῆταί τις, μὴ ἀποβαίνη δὲ κατὰ τὸ συμφέρον τῆς πρὸς ἀλλήλους κοινωνίας, οὐκέτι τοῦτο τὴν τοῦ δικαίου φύσιν ἔχει. Κἂν μεταπίπτη τὸ κατὰ τὸ δίκαιον συμφέρον, χρόνον δέ τινα εἰς τὴν πρόληψιν ἐναρμόττη, οὐδὲν ἧττον ἐκεῖνον τὸν χρόνον ἦν δίκαιον τοῖς μὴ φωναῖς κεναῖς ἑαυτοὺς συνταράττουσιν ἀλλ᾿ εἰς τὰ πράγματα βλέπουσιν.

XXXVIII. Ἔνθα μὴ καινῶν γενομένων τῶν περιεστώτων πραγμάτων ἀνεφάνη μὴ ἐναρμόττοντα εἰς τὴν πρόληψιν τὰ νομισθέντα δίκαια ἐπ᾿ αὐτῶν τῶν ἔργων, οὐκ ἦν ταῦτα δίκαια. Ἔνθα δὲ καινῶν γενομένων τῶν πραγμάτων οὐκέτι συνέφερε τὰ αὐτὰ δίκαια κείμενα, ἐνταῦθα δὲ τότε μὲν ἦν δίκαι, ὅτε συνέφερεν εἰς τὴν πρὸς

XXXVII. Among actions which are sanctioned as just by law, that which is proved on examination to be of advantage in the requirements of men's dealings with one another, has the guarantee of justice, whether it is the same for all or not. But if a man makes a law and it does not turn out to lead to advantage in men's dealings with each other, then it no longer has the essential nature of justice. And even if the advantage in the matter of justice shifts from one side to the other, but for a while accords with the general concept, it is none the less just for that period in the eyes of those who do not confound themselves with empty sounds but look to the actual facts.

XXXVIII. Where, provided the circumstances have not been altered, actions which were considered just, have been shown not to accord with the general concept in actual practice, then they are not just. But where, when circumstances have changed, the same actions which were sanctioned as just no longer lead to advantage, there

ἀλλήλους κοινωνίαν τῶν συμπολιτευομέ-
νων· ὕστερον δ᾽ οὐκ ἦν ἔτι δίκαια, ὅτε μὴ
συνέφερεν.

XXXIX. Ὁ τὸ μὴ θαρροῦν ἀπὸ τῶν ἔξωθεν ἄρι-
στα συστησάμενος οὗτος τὰ μὲν δυνατὰ
ὁμόφυλα κατεσκευάσατο· τὰ δὲ μὴ δυνατὰ οὐκ ἀλλόφυλά γε· ὅσα δὲ μηδὲ τοῦτο
δυνατὸς ἦν, ἀνεπίμικτος ἐγένετο, καὶ ἐξωρί-
σατο ὅσα τοῦτ᾽ ἐλυσιτέλει πράττειν.

XL. Ὅσοι τὴν δύναμιν ἔσχον τοῦ τὸ θαρρεῖν
μάλιστα ἐκ τῶν ὁμορούντων παρασκευά-
σασθαι, οὗτοι καὶ ἐβίωσαν μετ᾽ ἀλλήλων ἥ-
διστα τὸ βεβαιότατον πίστωμα ἔχοντες, καὶ
πληρεστάτην οἰκειότητα ἀπολαβόντες οὐκ
ὠδύραντο ὡς πρὸς ἔλεον τὴν τοῦ τελευτή-
σαντος προκαταστροφήν.

they were just at the time when they were of advantage for the dealings of fellow-citizens with one another, but subsequently they are no longer just, when no longer of advantage.

XXXIX. The man who has best ordered the element of disquiet arising from external circumstances has made those things that he could akin to himself and the rest at least not alien: but with all to which he could not do even this, he has refrained from mixing, and has expelled from his life all which it was of advantage to treat thus.

XL. As many as possess the power to procure complete immunity from their neighbours, these also live most pleasantly with one another, since they have the most certain pledge of security, and after they have enjoyed the fullest intimacy, they do not lament the previous departure of a dead friend, as though he were to be pitied.

Ἐπίκουρου Προσφώνησις

Vatican Collection

Epicurus' Exhortation

I. = *Κύριαι Δόξαι* I.

II. = *Κύριαι Δόξαι* II.

III. = *Κύριαι Δόξαι* IV.

IV. Πᾶσα ἀλγηδὼν εὐκαταφρόνητος· ἡ γὰρ
σύντονον ἔχουσα τὸ πονοῦν σύντομον ἔχει
τὸν χρόνον, ἡ δὲ χρονίζουσα περὶ τὴν σάρκα ἀβληχρὸν ἔχει τὸν πόνον.

V. = *Κύριαι Δόξαι* V.

VI. = *Κύριαι Δόξαι* XXXV.

VII. Ἀδικοῦντα λαθεῖν μὲν δύσκολον, πίστιν
δὲ λαβεῖν ὑπὲρ τοῦ λαθεῖν ἀδύνατον.

VIII. = *Κύριαι Δόξαι* XV.

IX. Κακὸν ἀνάγκη, ἀλλ᾽ οὐδεμία ἀνάγκη ζῆν
μετὰ ἀνάγκης.

IV. All bodily suffering is negligible: for that which causes acute pain has short duration, and that which endures long in the flesh causes but mild pain.

VII. It is hard for an evil-doer to escape detection, but to obtain security for escaping is impossible.

IX. Necessity is an evil, but there is no necessity to live under the control of necessity.

[X. Metrodorus. Μέμνησο ὅτι θνητὸς ὢν τῇ
φύσει καὶ λαβὼν χρόνον ὡρισμένον ἀνέβης
τοῖς περὶ φύσεως διαλογισμοῖς ἐπὶ τὴν ἀπει-
ρίαν καὶ τὸν αἰῶνα καὶ κατεῖδες
    τα τ᾽ ἐόντα τά τ᾽ ἐσσόμενα πρό τ᾽ ἐόντα.]

XI. Τῶν πλείστον ἀνθρώπων τὸ μὲν ἡσύχαζον
ναρκᾷ, τὸ δὲ κινούμενον λυττᾷ.

XII. = Κύριαι Δόξαι XVII.
XIII. = Κύριαι Δόξαι XXVII.

XIV. Γεγόναμεν ἅπαξ, δὶς οὐκ ἔστι γενέσθαι·
δεῖ δὲ τὸν αἰῶνα μηκέτ᾽ εἶναι· σὺ δὲ οὐκ ὢν
τῆς αὔριον <κύριος> ἀναβάλλῃ τὸ χαῖρον·
ὁ δὲ βίος μελλησμῷ παραπόλλυται καὶ εἷς
ἕκαστος ἡμῶν ἀσχολούμενος ἀποθνήσκει.

XV. Ἤθη ὥσπερ τὰ ἡμῶν αὐτῶν ἴδια τιμῶμεν,
ἄν τε χρηστὰ ἔχωμεν καὶ ὑπὸ τῶν ἀνθρώπων ζηλώμεθα, ἄν τε μή· οὕτω χρὴ <τὰ> τῶν
πέλας, ἂν ἐπιεικεῖς ὦσιν.

[X. Remember that you are of mortal nature and have a limited time to live and have devoted yourself to discussions on nature for all time and eternity and have seen 'things that are now and are to come and have been'.]

XI. For most men rest is stagnation and activity madness.

XIV. We are born once and cannot be born twice, but for all time must be no more. But you, who are not <master> of tomorrow, postpone your happiness: life is wasted in procrastination and each one of us dies without allowing himself leisure.

XV. We value our characters as something peculiar to ourselves, whether they are good and we are esteemed by men, or not; so ought we to value the characters of others, if they are well-disposed to us.

XVI. Οὐδεὶς βλέπων τὸ κακὸν αἱρεῖται αὐτό, ἀλλὰ δελεασθεὶς ὡς ἀγαθῷ πρὸς τὸ μεῖζον αὐτοῦ κακὸν ἐθηρεύθη.

XVII. Οὐ νέος μακαριστὸς ἀλλὰ γέρων βεβιωκὼς καλῶς· ὁ γὰρ νέος <ἐν> ἀκμῇ πολὺς ὑπὸ τῆς τύχης ἑτεροφρονῶν πλάζεται· ὁ δὲ γέρων καθάπερ ἐν λιμένι τῷ γήρᾳ καθώρμικεν τὰ πρότερον δυσελπιστούμενα τῶν ἀγαθῶν ἀσφαλεῖ κατακλείσας χάριτι.

XVIII. Ἀφαιρουμένης προσόψεως καὶ ὁμιλίας καὶ συναναστροφῆς ἐκλύεται τὸ ἐρωτικόν πάθος.

XIX. Τοῦ γεγονότος ἀμνήμων ἀγαθοῦ γέρων τήμερον γεγένηται.

XX. = Κύριαι Δόξαι XXIX

XXI. Οὐ βιαστέον τὴν φύσιν ἀλλὰ πειστέον· πεισόμεθα δὲ τάς <τ'> ἀναγκαίας ἐπιθυ-

XVI. No one when he sees evil deliberately chooses it, but is enticed by it as being good in comparison with a greater evil and so pursues it.

XVII. It is not the young man who should be thought happy, but an old man who has lived a good life. For the young man at the helght of his powers is unstable and is carried this way and that by fortune, like a headlong stream. But the old man has come to anchor in old age as though in port, and the good things for which before he hardly hoped he has brought into safe harbourage in his grateful recollections.

XVIII. Remove sight, association and contact, and the passion of love is at an end.

XIX. Forgetting the good that has been he has become old this very day.

XXI. We must not violate nature, but obey her; and we shall obey her if we fulfil the necessary

μίας ἐκπληροῦντες τάς τε φυσικὰς ἂν μὴ
βλάπτωσι, τὰς δὲ βλαβερὰς πικρῶς ἐλέγ-
χοντες.

XXII = *Κύριαι Δόξαι* XIX

XXIII. Πᾶσα φιλία δι᾽ ἑαυτὴν αἱρετή· ἀρχὴν
δ᾽ εἴληφεν ἀπὸ τῆς ὠφελείας.

XXIV. Ἐνύπνια οὐκ ἔλαχε φύσιν θείαν οὐδὲ
μαντικὴν δύναμιν, ἀλλὰ γίνεται κατὰ ἔμ-
πτωσιν εἰδώλων.

XXV. Ἡ πενία μετρουμένη τῷ τῆς φύσεως
τέλει μέγας ἐστὶ πλοῦτος· πλοῦτος δὲ μὴ
ὁριζόμενος μεγάλη ἐστὶ πενία.

XXVI. Δεῖ διαλαβεῖν ὅτι καὶ ὁ πολὺς λόγος καὶ
ὁ βραχὺς εἰς τὸ αὐτὸ συντείνει τέλος.

XXVII. Ἐπὶ μὲν τῶν ἄλλων ἐπιτηδευμάτων μό-
λις τελειωθεῖσιν ὁ καρπὸς ἔρχεται, ἐπὶ δὲ φιλοσοφίας συντρέχει τῇ γνώσει τὸ τερπνόν·

desires and also the physical, if they bring no harm to us, but sternly reject the harmful.

XXIII. All friendship is desirable in itself, though it starts from the need of help.

XXIV. Dreams have no divine character nor any prophetic force, but they originate from the influx of Images.

XXV. Poverty, when measured by the natural purpose of life, is great wealth, but unlimited wealth is great poverty.

XXVI. You must understand that whether the discourse be long or short it tends to the same end.

XXVII. In all other occupations the fruit comes painfully after completion, but in philosophy pleasure goes hand in hand with knowledge; for enjoyment does not follow comprehension,

οὐ γὰρ μετὰ μάθησιν ἀπόλαυσις, ἀλλὰ ἅμα μάθησις καὶ ἀπόλαυσις.

XXVIII. Οὔτε τοὺς προχείρους εἰς φιλίαν οὔτε τοὺς ὀκνηροὺς δοκιμαστέον· δεῖ δὲ καὶ παρακινδυνεῦσαι χάριν φιλίας.

XXIX. Παρρησίᾳ γὰρ ἔγωγε χρώμενος φυσιολογῶν χρησμοδεῖν τὰ συμφέροντα πᾶσιν ἀνθρώποις μᾶλλον ἂν βουλοίμην κἂν μηδεὶς μέλλῃ συνήσειν, ἢ συγκατατιθέμενος ταῖς δόξαις καρποῦσθαι τὸν πυκνὸν παραπίπτοντα παρὰ τῶν πολλῶν ἔπαινον.

[XXX. Metrodorus. Ἑτοιμάζονταί τινες διὰ βίου τὰ πρὸς τὸν βίον, οὐ συνορῶντες ὡς πᾶσιν ἡμῖν θανάσιμον ἐγκέχυται τὸ τῆς γενέσεως φάρμακον.]

XXXI. Πρὸς μὲν τἄλλα δυνατὸν ἀσφάλειαν πορίσασθαι, χάριν δὲ θανάτου πάντες ἄνθρωποι πόλιν ἀτείχιστον οἰκοῦμεν.

but comprehension and enjoyment are simultaneous.

XXVIII. We must not approve either those who are always ready for friendship, or those who hang back, but for friendship's sake we must even run risks.

XXIX. In investigating nature I would prefer to speak openly and like an oracle to give answers serviceable to all mankind, even though no one should understand me, rather than to conform to popular opinions and so win the praise freely scattered by the mob.

[XXX. Some men throughout their lives gather together the means of life, for they do not see that the draught swallowed by all of us at birth is a draught of death.]

XXXI. Against all else it is possible to provide security, but as against death all of us mortals alike dwell in an unfortified city.

XXXII. Ὁ τοῦ σοφοῦ σεβασμὸς ἀγαθὸν μέγα τῶν σεβομένων ἐστί.

XXXIII. Σαρκὸς φωνὴ τὸ μὴ πεινῆν, τὸ μὴ δι-ψῆν, τὸ μὴ ῥιγοῦν. Ταῦτα γὰρ ἔχων τις καὶ ἐλπίζων ἕξειν κἂν <Διὶ> ὑπὲρ εὐδαιμονίας μαχέσαιτο.

XXXIV. Οὐχ οὕτως χρείαν ἔχομεν τῆς χρείας παρὰ τῶν φίλων ὡς τῆς πίστεως τῆς περί τῆς χρείας.

XXXV. Οὐ δεῖ λυμαίνεσθαι τὰ παρόντα τῶν ἀπόντων ἐπιθυμία, ἀλλ᾽ ἐπιλογίζεσθαι ὅτι καὶ ταῦτα τῶν εὐκταίων ἦν.

[XXXVI. Ὁ Ἐπικούρου βίος τοῖς τῶν ἄλλων συγκρινόμενος ἕνεκεν ἡμερότητος καὶ αὐ-ταρκείας μῦθος ἂν νομισθείη.]

XXXVII. Ἀσθενὴς ἡ φύσις ἐστὶ πρὸς τὸ κακόν, οὐ πρὸς τὸ ἀγαθόν· ἡδοναῖς μὲν γὰρ σώζε-ται, ἀλγηδόσι δὲ διαλύεται.

XXXII. The veneration of the Wise man is a great blessing to those who venerate him.

XXXIII. The flesh cries out to be saved from hunger, thirst and cold. For if a man possess this safety and hope to possess it, he might rival even Zeus in happiness.

XXXIV. It is not so much our friends' help that helps us as the confidence of their help.

XXXV. We should not spoil what we have by desiring what we have not, but remember that what we have too was the gift of fortune.

[XXXVI. Epicurus' life when compared to other men's in respect of gentleness and self-sufficiency might be thought a mere legend.]

XXXVII. Nature is weak towards evil, not towards good: because it is saved by pleasures, but destroyed by pains.

XXXVIII. Μικρός παντάπασιν, ᾧ πολλαὶ αἰτίαι
εὔλογοι εἰς ἐξαγωγὴν βίου.

XXXIX. Οὔθ ὁ τὴν χρείαν ἐπιζητῶν διὰ παντός
φίλος οὔθ ὁ μηδέποτε συνάπτων· ὃ μὲν
γὰρ καπηλεύει τῇ χάριτι τὴν ἀμοιβήν, ὃ
δὲ ἀποκόπτει τὴν περὶ τοῦ μέλλοντος εὐελ-
πιστίαν.

XL. Ὁ λέγων πάντα κατ᾽ ἀνάγκην γίνεσθαι
οὐδὲν ἐγκαλεῖν ἔχει τῷ λέγοντι μὴ πάντα
κατ᾽ ἀνάγκην γίνεσθαι· αὐτὸ γὰρ τοῦτό φησι κατ᾽ ἀνάγκην γίνεσθαι.

XLI. Γελᾶν ἅμα δεῖν καὶ φιλοσοφεῖν καὶ οἰκο-
νομεῖν καὶ τοῖς λοιποῖς οἰκειώμασι χρῆσθαι
καὶ μηδαμῇ λήγειν τὰς ἐκ τῆς ὀρθῆς φιλοσοφίας φωνὰς ἀφίεντας.

XLII. Ὁ αὐτὸς χρόνος καὶ γενέσεως τοῦ μεγί-
στου ἀγαθοῦ καὶ ἀπολαύσεως.

XXXVIII. He is a little man in all respects who has many good reasons for quitting life.

XXXIX. He is no friend who is continually asking for help, nor he who never associates help with friendship. For the former barters kindly feeling for a practical return and the latter destroys the hope of good in the future.

XL. The man who says that all things come to pass by necessity cannot criticize one who denies that all things come to pass by necessity: for he admits that this too happens of necessity.

XLI. We must laugh and philosophize at the same time and do our household duties and employ our other faculties, and never cease proclaiming the sayings of the true philosophy.

XLII. The greatest blessing is created and enjoyed at the same moment.

XLIII. Φιλαργυρεῖν ἄδικα μὲν ἀσεβές, δίκαια
δὲ αἰσχρόν· ἀπρεπὲς γὰρ ῥυπαρῶς φείδε-
σθαι καὶ μετὰ τοῦ δικαίου.

XLIV. Ὁ σοφὸς εἰς τὰ ἀναγκαῖα συγκαθεὶς
μᾶλλον ἐπίσταται μεταδιδόναι ἢ μεταλαμ-
βάνειν· τηλικοῦτον αὐταρκείας εὗρε θησαυ-
ρόν.

XLV. Οὐ κόμπου οὐδὲ φωνῆς ἐργαστικοὺς
οὐδὲ τὴν περιμάχητον παρὰ τοῖς πολλοῖς
παιδείαν ἐνδεικνυμένους φυσιολογία παρασκευάζει, ἀλλὰ σοβαροὺς καὶ αὐτάρκεις
καὶ ἐπὶ τοῖς ἰδίοις ἀγαθοῖς, οὐκ ἐπὶ τοῖς τῶν
πραγμάτων μέγα φρονοῦντας.

XLVI. Τὰς φαύλας συνηθείας ὥσπερ ἄνδρας
πονηροὺς πολὺν χρόνον μέγα βλάψαντας
τελείως ἐκδιώκωμεν.

[XLVII. Metrodorus. Προκατείλημμαί σε, ὦ τύχη, καὶ πᾶσαν σὴν παρείσδυσιν ἐνέφραξα.
Καὶ οὔτε σοὶ οὔτε ἄλλῃ οὐδεμίᾳ περιστάσει

XLIII. The love of money, if unjustly gained, is impious, and, if justly, shameful; for it is unseemly to be merely parsimonious even with justice on one's side.

XLIV. The wise man when he has accommodated himself to straits knows better how to give than to receive: so great is the treasure of self-sufficiency which he has discovered.

XLV. The study of nature does not make men productive of boasting or bragging nor apt to display that culture which is the object of rivalry with the many, but highspirited and self-sufficient, taking pride in the good things of their own minds and not of their circumstances.

XLVI. Our bad habits, like evil men who have long done us great harm, let us utterly drive from us.

[XLVII. I have anticipated thee, Fortune, and entrenched myself against all thy secret attacks.

δώσομεν ἑαυτοὺς ἐκδότους· ἀλλ᾽ ὅταν ἡ-
μᾶς τὸ χρεὼν ἐξάγῃ, μέγα προσπτύσαντες
τῷ ζῆν καὶ τοῖς αὐτῷ κενῶς περιπλατ-
τομένοις ἄπιμεν ἐκ τοῦ ζῆν μετὰ καλοῦ
παιῶνος ἐπιφωνοῦντες ὡς εὖ ἡμῖν βεβίω-
ται.]

XLVIII. Πειρᾶσθαι τὴν ὑστέραν τῆς προτέρας
κρείττω ποιεῖν, ἕως ἂν ἐν ὁδῷ ὦμεν· ἐπειδὰν δ᾽ ἐπὶ πέρας ἔλθωμεν, ὁμαλῶς εὐφραί-
νεσθαι.

XLIX. = *Κύριαι Δόξαι* XII.
L. = *Κύριαι Δόξαι* VIII.

LI. Πυνθάνομαί σου τὴν κατὰ σάρκα κίνησιν
ἀφθονώτερον διακεῖσθαι πρὸς τὴν τῶν ἀ-
φροδισίων ἔντευξιν. Σὺ δὲ ὅταν μήτε τοὺς
νόμους καταλύσῃς μήτε τὰ καλῶς ἔθη κείμενα κινῇς μήτε τῶν πλησίον τινὰ λυπῇς μήτε
τὴν σάρκα καταξαίνῃς μήτε τὰ ἀναγκαῖα
καταναλίσκῃς, χρῶ ὡς βούλει τῇ σεαυτοῦ
προαιρέσει. Ἀμήχανον μέντοι γε τὸ μὴ οὐχ

And we will not give ourselves up as captives to thee or to any other circumstance; but when it is time for us to go, spitting contempt on life and on those who here vainly cling to it, we will leave life crying aloud in a glorious triumph-song that we have lived well.]

XLVIII. We must try to make the end of the journey better than the beginning, as long as we are journeying, but when we come to the end, we must be happy and content.

LI. You tell me that the stimulus of thie flesh makes you too prone to the pleasures of love. Provided that you do not break the laws or good customs and do not distress any of your neighbours or do harm to your body or squander your pittance, you may indulge your inclination as you please. Yet it is impossible not to come up against one or other of these barriers: for the

ἑνί γέ τινι τούτων συνέχεσθαι· ἀφροδίσια
γὰρ οὐδέποτε ὤνησεν· ἀγαπητὸν δὲ εἰ μὴ
ἔβλαψεν.

LII. Ἡ φιλία περιχορεύει τὴν οἰκουμένην κη-
ρύττουσα δὴ πᾶσιν ἡμῖν ἐγείρεσθαι ἐπὶ τὸν
μακαρισμόν.

LIII. Οὐδενὶ φθονητέον· ἀγαθοὶ γὰρ οὐκ ἄξιοι
φθόνου, πονηροὶ δὲ ὅσῳ ἂν μᾶλλον εὐτυ-
χῶσι, τοσούτῳ μᾶλλον αὐτοῖς λυμαίνονται.

LIV. Οὐ προσποιεῖσθαι δεῖ φιλοσοφεῖν, ἀλλ' ὄ-
ντως φιλοσοφεῖν· οὐ γὰρ προσδεόμεθα τοῦ
δοκεῖν ὑγιαίνειν, ἀλλὰ τοῦ κατ' ἀλήθειαν
ὑγιαίνειν.

LV. Θεραπευτέον τὰς συμφορὰς τῇ τῶν ἀπολ-
λυμένων χάριτι καὶ τῷ γινώσκειν ὅτι οὐκ
ἔστιν ἄπρακτον ποιῆσαι τὸ γεγονός.

LVI-LVII. Ἀλγεῖ μὲν ὁ σοφὸς οὐ μᾶλλον στρε-
βλούμενος <αὐτὸς ἢ ὁρῶν στρεβλούμε-

pleasures of love never profited a man and he is lucky if they do him no harm.

LII. Friendship goes dancing round the world proclaiming to us all to awake to the praises of a happy life.

LIII. We must envy no one: for the good do not deserve envy and the bad, the more they prosper, the more they injure themselves.

LIV. We must not pretend to study philosophy, but study it in reality: for it is not the appearance of health that we need, but real health.

LV. We must heal our misfortunes by the grateful recollection of what has been and by the recognition that it is impossible to make undone what has been done.

LVI-LVII. The wise man is not more pained when being tortured <himself, than when seeing> his friend <tortured>: but if his friend does him

νον> τὸν φίλον... ὁ βίος αὐτοῦ πᾶς δι᾽ ἀπι-
στίαν συγχυθήσεται καὶ ἀνακεχαιστισμέ-
νος ἔσται.

LVIII. Ἐκλυτέον ἑαυτοὺς ἐκ τοῦ περὶ τὰ ἐγκύ-
κλια καὶ πολιτικὰ δεσμωτηρίου.

LIX. Ἄπληστον οὐ γαστήρ, ὥσπερ οἱ πολλοί
φασιν, ἀλλὰ δόξα ψευδὴς ὑπὲρ τοῦ γαστρὸς
ἀορίστου πληρώματος.

LX. Πᾶς ὥσπερ ἄρτι γεγονὼς ἐκ τοῦ ζῆν ἀπέρχεται.

LXI. Καλλίστη καὶ ἡ τῶν πλησίον ὄψις, τῆς πρώ-
της συγγενείας ὁμονοούσης, ἢ πολλὴν εἰς
τοῦτο ποιουμένη σπουδήν.

LXII. Εἰ γὰρ κατὰ τὸ δέον ὀργαὶ γίγνονται τοῖς
γεννήσασι πρὸς τὰ ἔκγονα, μάταιον δή-
πουθέν ἐστι τὸ ἀντιτείνειν καὶ μὴ παραι-
τεῖσθαι συγγνώμης τυχεῖν· εἰ δὲ μὴ κατὰ τὸ
δέον ἀλλὰ ἀλογώτερον, γελοῖον πάνυ τὸ

wrong, his whole life will be confounded by distrust and completely upset.

LVIII. We must release ourselves from the prison of affairs and politics.

LIX. It is not the stomach that is insatiable, as is generally said, but the false opinion that the stomach needs an unlimited amount to fill it.

LX. Every man passes out of life as though he had just been born.

LXI. Most beautiful too is the sight of those near and dear to us, when our original kinship makes us of one mind; for such sight is a great incitement to this end.

LXII. Now it parents are justly angry with their children, it is certainly useless to fight against it and not to ask for pardon; but if their anger is unjust and irrational, it is quite ridiculous to add fuel to their irrational passion by nursing one's

προσεκκαίειν τὴν ἀλογίαν θυμοκατοχοῦντα, καὶ μὴ ζητεῖν μεταθεῖναι κατ᾿ ἄλλους τρόπους εὐγνωμονοῦντα.

LXIII. Ἔστι καὶ ἐν λιτότητι μεθόριος, ἧς ὁ ἀνεπιλόγιστος παραπλήσιόν τι πάσχει τῷ δ᾿ ἀοριστίαν ἐκπίπτοντι.

LXIV. Ἀκολουθεῖν δεῖ τὸν παρὰ τῶν ἄλλων ἔπαινον αὐτόματον, ἡμᾶς δὲ γενέσθαι περὶ τὴν ἡμῶν ἰατρείαν.

LXV. Μάταιόν ἐστι παρὰ θεῶν αἰτεῖσθαι ἅ τις ἑαυτῷ χορηγῆσαι ἱκανός ἐστι.

LXVI. Συμπαθῶμεν τοῖς φίλοις οὐ θρηνοῦντες ἀλλὰ φροντίζοντες.

LXVII. Ἐλεύθερος βίος οὐ δύναται κτήσαθαι χρήματα πολλὰ διὰ τὸ πρᾶγμα <μὴ> ῥάδιον εἶναι χωρὶς θητείας ὄχλων ἢ δυναστῶν, ἀλλὰ <σὺν> συνεχεῖ δαψιλείᾳ πάντα κέκτηται· ἂν δέ που καὶ τύχῃ χρημάτων πολλῶν,

own indignation, and not to attempt to turn aside their wrath in other ways by gentleness.

LXIII. Frugality too has a limit, and the man who disregards it is in like case with him who errs through excess.

LXIV. Praise from others must come unasked: we must concern ourselves with the healing of our own lives.

LXV. It is vain to ask of the gods what a man is capable of supplying for himself.

LXVI. Let us show our feeling for our lost friends not by lamentation but by meditation.

LXVII. A free life cannot acquire many possessions, because this is not easy to do without servility to mobs or monarchs, yet it possesses all things in unfailing abundance; and if by chance it obtains many possessions, it is easy to distribute them so as to win the gratitude of neighbours.

καὶ ταῦτα ῥᾳδίως ἂν εἰς τὴν τοῦ πλησίον εὔ-
νοιαν διαμέτρησαι.

LXVIII. Οὐδὲν ἱκανὸν ᾧ ὀλίγον τὸ ἱκανόν.

LXIX. Τὸ τῆς ψυχῆς ἀχάριστον λίχνον ἐποίησε
τὸ ζῷον εἰς ἄπειρον τῶν ἐν διαίτῃ ποικιλ-
μάτων.

LXX. Μηδὲν σοι ἐν βίῳ πραχθείη ὁ φόβον πα-
ρέξει σοι, εἰ γνωσθήσεται τῷ πλησίον.

LXXI. Πρὸς πάσας τὰς ἐπιθυμίας προσακτέον
τὸ ἐπερώτημα τοῦτο· τί μοι γενήσεται ἂν
τελεσθῇ τὸ κατὰ τὴν ἐπιθυμίαν ἐπιζητού-
μενον, καὶ τί ἐὰν μὴ τελεσθῇ;

LXXII. = *Κύριαι Δόξαι* XIII.

LXXIII. Καὶ τὸ γεγενῆσθαί τινας ἀλγηδόνας
περὶ σῶμα λυσιτελεῖ πρὸς φυλακὴν τῶν ὁ-
μοειδῶν.

LXVIII. Nothing is suflicient for him to whom what is suflicient seems little.

LXIX. The ungrateful greed of the soul makes the creature everlastingly desire varieties of dainty food.

LXX. Let nothing be done in your life, which will cause you fear if it becomes known to your neighbour.

LXXI. Every desire must be confronted with this question: what will happen to me, if the object of my desire is accomplished and what if it is not?

LXXIII. The occurrence of certain bodily pains assists us in guarding against others like them.

LXXIV. Ἐν φιλολόγῳ συζητήσει πλεῖον ἤνυσεν ὁ ἡττηθείς, καθ᾽ ὃ προσέμαθεν.

LXXV. Εἰς τὰ παρῳχηκότα ἀγαθὰ ἀχάριστος φωνὴ ἡ λέγουσα "Τέλος ὅρα μακροῦ βίου".

LXXVI. Τοιοῦτος εἶ γηράσκων ὁποῖον ἐγὼ παραινῶ, καὶ διέγνωκας ὁποῖόν ἐστι τὸ ἑαυτῷ φιλοσοφῆσαι καὶ οἷον τὸ τῇ Ἑλλάδι· συγχαίρω σοι.

LXXVII. Τῆς αὐταρκείας καρπὸς μέγιστος ἐλευθερία.

LXXVIII. Ὁ γενναῖος περὶ σοφίαν καὶ φιλίαν μάλιστα γίγνεται· ὧν τὸ μέν ἐστι θνητὸν ἀγαθόν, τὸ δ᾽ ἀθάνατον.

LXXIX. Ὁ ἀτάραχος ἑαυτῷ καὶ ἑτέρῳ ἀόχλητος.

LXXIV. In a philosophical discussion he who is worsted gains more in proportion as he learns more.

LXXV. Ungrateful towards the blessings of the past is the saying, 'Wait till the end of a long life'.

LXXVI. You are in your old age just such as I urge you to be, and you have seen the difference between studying philosophy for oneself and proclaiming it to Greece at large: I rejoice with you.

LXXVII. The greatest fruit of self-sufficiency is freedom.

LXXVIII. The noble soul occupies itself with wisdom and friendship: of these the one is a mortal good, the other immortal.

LXXIX. The man who is serene causes no disturbance to himself or to another.

LXXX. Ἔστιν πρώτη σωτηρίας μοῖρα τῆς ἡλι-
κίας τήρησις καὶ φυλακὴ τῶν πάντα μολυ-
νόντων κατὰ τὰς ἐπιθυμίας τὰς οἰστρώδεις.

LXXXI. Οὐ λύει τὴν τῆς ψυχῆς ταραχὴν οὐδὲ
τὴν ἀξιόλογον ἀπογεννᾷ χαρὰν οὔτε πλοῦτος ὑπάρχων ὁ μέγιστος οὔθ᾽ ἡ παρὰ τοῖς
πολλοῖς τιμὴ καὶ περίβλεψις οὔτ᾽ ἄλλο τι
τῶν παρὰ τὰς ἀδιορίστους αἰτίας.

LXXX. The first measure of security is to watch over one's youth and to guard against what makes havoc of all by means of pestering desires.

LXXXI. The disturbance of the soul cannot be ended nor true joy created either by the possession of the greatest wealth or by honour and respect in the eyes of the mob or by anything else that is associated with causes of unlimited desire.

Notes

LETTER TO MENOECEUS

The third letter, written to Epicurus' disciple Menoeceus, is a brief exposition of the philosopher's moral theory. It starts with a reiteration of the two fundamental conditions of the moral life, the right understanding of the nature of the gods and the freedom from the fear of death, after which the rest of the letter is devoted to a clear and logical statement of Epicurus' view that pleasure is the end of life and of the sense in which this is to be understood.

The letter is not intended, like that of Herodotus, for the use of advanced students, but is a simple and straightforward exposition for the general reader. It is in fact an 'exoteric' work, as Aristotle might have called it, and as such, contains far more references than the other letters to rival theories and popular views.

The common ideas as to the nature and activities of the gods are passed in review and their weakness is exposed, popular notions as to the terrible nature of death are condemned, and vulgar conceptions of the character of true pleasure are refuted. References are made, implicitly or explicitly, to ideas of Plato, of the Cyrenaics, of the Stoics, of Theognis, and possibly of Epicharmus and Mimnermus.

It is clear that however devoted a disciple Menoeceus may have been, the letter was intended to reach a wider public who might still be under the influence of an erroneous philosophy or of the unsupported maxims and opinions of popular thought.

PRINCIPAL DOCTRINES

The Κύριαι Δόξαι are a series of brief aphorisms dealing with Epicurus' ethical theory, and in particular with the conditions requisite for the tranquil life of the Epicurean philosopher.

They are introduced by Diogenes Laertius as 'the crown (κολοφῶνα) of all Epicurus' writings and of the philosophic life', and are quoted by name and with unmistakable references by Philodemus and the Epicurean writers in the Herculanean rolls, who speak of

'those who write against the Κύριαι Δόξαι'. Plutarch, Diodorus, and Lucian refer to them under the same title. Cicero in one passage appears to translate the title as 'Authoritative Sayings', in another as 'Selected Sayings', but undoubtedly regards them as the work of Epicurus. There can then be no doubt that in antiquity the Κύριαι Δόξαι were looked upon as an authentic work of the Master deserving very special esteem and consideration.

The Κύριαι δόξαι is a practical manual of guidance for life intended for the professed Epicurean; it does not claim to be a consecutive treatise on ethics, but deals successively with the various topics of importance for its own practical end. With all the ancient testimony which we have in its favour, there seems no sound reason for doubting that it is the work of Epicurus himself, nor, if its character be rightly understood, does its working out seem unworthy of him or more appropriate to an unintelligent compiler.

The picture of the 'true Epicurean' which it represents is consistent with what we learn from other sources, and in particular from the third letter, to Menoeceus. It is based on a relentless working out of the idea of pleasure as the end of life (which ts characteristically never stated in the aphorisms), and though in some details, such as the conceptions of justice and

friendship, its individualism strikes the reader as almost incredibly cynical, yet the image of the tranquil life has its strong attractions, and the vision of the Epicurean community with which the series concludes has a considerable beauty of its own. We may safely regard the Principal Doctrines as Ratae, the authentic dicta of their Master, and also as Selectae in the sense that they do not attempt to cover the whole field of ethics, but only to lay down the conditions for the true Epicurean life.

VATICAN COLLECTION

It is a collection of eighty aphorisms discovered in 1888 by C. Wotke in a Vatican manuscript (Codex Vaticanus gr. 1950) and published by him in *Wiener Studien*, 1888, pp 191 ff. The manuscript, which is of the fourteenth century, is a miscellany containing works of Xenophon, the *Thoughts* of Marcus Aurelius, Epictetus' *Manual*, and other works.

The present collection is headed Ἐπίκουρου Προσφώνησις (Epicurus' Exhortation). Some of the sayings, denoted in the text by square brackets, came not from Epicurus but from his disciples, in several instances from Metrodorus. About twenty of them were already

known, several being quotations from the Κύριαι Δό-ξαι. The rest were probably selected from various works of Epicurus, not a few of them seeming to be quotations from private letters.

The collection deals almost wholly with the moral theory of Epicurus and adds on many points to our knowledge of the system.

Vain is the word of a philosopher
which does not heal any suffering of man.
For just as there is no profit in medicine
if it does not expel the diseases of the body,
so there is no profit in philosophy either,
if it does not expel the suffering of the mind.

EPICURUS

ALSO FROM
AIORA PRESS:

Myths Behind Words

GREEK MYTHOLOGY
IN ENGLISH WORDS AND EXPRESSIONS

Compiled by Alexander Zaphiriou
Illustrated by Panagiotis Stavropoulos

Like the constellations in the sky, words such as 'aphro-disiac', 'hubris', 'museum', 'galaxy' and 'mentor' each contain within them a story, if only you knew to look closely. This collection retells the myths behind common words and expressions in English, bringing to life the heroes, monsters and gods whose deeds and battles have left a hidden mark on our language.

AN ANTHOLOGY

Words of Wisdom from Ancient Greece

Translated by Alexander Zaphiriou
Illustrated by Panagiotis Stavropoulos

BILINGUAL EDITION

Words of Wisdom from Ancient Greece gathers the best of a thousand years of philosophy, history and literature, in a compilation of writing spanning from 800 BCE to 200 AD. This survey of ancient wisdom offers guidance for a life well lived from luminaries of Greece's legendary past.

HIPPOCRATES

Aphorisms

Translated by W.H.S. Jones

BILINGUAL EDITION

Hippocrates of Kos is credited with being the first healer to separate the discipline of medicine from religion, arguing that disease was not a punishment inflicted by the gods but rather the product of environmental factors, diet and lifestyle. The tradition is that Hippocrates composed the *Aphorisms* in his old age as a summary of his vast experience.

EPICTETUS

Manual
on the Art of Living

Translated by P.E. Matheson

BILINGUAL EDITION

'Of all existing things, some are in our power, and others
are not in our power.' So begins the *Manual* or *Enchirid-
ion* of Epictetus, a collection of precepts that together
provide a powerful philosophy for daily life. The *Manual*,
considered to be the pinnacle of Stoic philosophy, ad-
dresses living with integrity, self-management and per-
sonal freedom.

PYTHAGORAS

The Golden Verses

Translated by David Connolly

BILINGUAL EDITION

The essence of Pythagoras' teachings is contained in *The
Golden Verses*, seventy-one verses as guidelines on how
to live. Functioning as admonitions, they link the human
with the divine element and determine the point at
which both elements converge to reveal how we might
ourselves attain this supreme virtue in our everyday lives.